SCOTLAND IN COLOUR

1   The Castle of Macleod of Dunvegan, Isle of Skye

SCOTLAND IN COLOUR

By
Moray McLaren

With 32 Photographs
in Colour by
A. F. Kersting

Foreword by
Sir Compton Mackenzie

L o n d o n
B. T. BATSFORD LTD

First Published 1954

Made and printed in Great Britain by
WILLIAM CLOWES AND SONS, LIMITED
for the publishers B. T. BATSFORD LTD
4 FITZHARDINGE STREET, PORTMAN SQUARE,
LONDON W.I.

FOREWORD

by SIR COMPTON MACKENZIE

I THINK it is true to say that the average visitor does not associate Scotland predominantly with colour, and that is because the great majority of visitors see Scotland in August, when in most years the weather is wet. There is, of course, the heather, but purple is a colour that demands the sun; otherwise it intensifies the melancholy of a prospect. Charles Dickens in *The Pickwick Papers* was lyrical about the beauty of the English countryside in August, but, wet or fine, I should argue that this is the least attractive of the summer months in England, so uniform and heavy is the prevailing green. In fact, I find August the dullest month for scenery anywhere in the British Isles.

It may seem extravagant to claim that the colour of the sea in the Outer Hebrides (and I believe in Shetland) is matchless in Europe except in the Aegean, but so it is. In the Outer Hebrides the colour on a calm day in midwinter can be more beautiful than any I have seen in the Aegean at any season. Nor need the traveller voyage to the Outer Isles for blue. I have sighted Loch Maree from Glen Docherty on a fine morning when the sun was still easterly making the finest zircon look dull.

Moray McLaren praises autumn in Scotland, and I shall not spoil his judicious rapture by expatiating upon that. Indeed, this foreword, like most forewords in my experience, is superfluous because the author has covered his ground with an eloquent agility that speaks for itself. I am surprised not by what he has left out but by the amount he has managed to include without confusing the reader.

Moreover, he has been very well served by the photographs in colour which his text accompanies; I do not recall a nicer presentation of the Scottish scene.

One of the pleasures of turning the pages of a book like this is the thought that many readers of it will not yet have seen the places it depicts, and I can envy those who for the first time will behold those places, as we who are old may sometimes with benevolence envy youth.

Spring, 1954.

7

2 Clouds over Ben Nevis seen from the village of Corpach on the north bend of Loch Eil

LIST OF ILLUSTRATIONS

3 Morning sun on Calton Hill, Edinburgh. Looking west from the Dugald Stewart monument

4   The view from Arthur's Seat across Edinburgh to the Firth of Forth, with the Palace of Holyroodhouse in the foreground

5   The upper reaches of the River Tweed near Tweedsmuir, Peeblesshire

I

ABOUT twenty-five years ago a young Scot in London was seized with a fit of home-sickness for his native country. He decided to try to express his feelings in the picaresque prose then fashionable in travel books, and set himself down in London to write about returning to Scotland. To stimulate his imagination, he placed himself in thought upon the summit of the Pentland Hills above Edinburgh, and, looking down over his native city and far beyond into the north, he fancied he saw the whole of Scotland before him. It was an act not only of imagination but of recollection; for this young man had spent much of his boyhood in and about these guardian hills of the capital of Scotland. "Hills of home" Stevenson had called them in a poem written in the last years of his life and from the other side of the world; and to this young journalist, alone in what was then to him the almost foreign city of London, they also were hills of home. At the mere thought of them as he tried to set down upon paper the feelings aroused in him by them, the roar of London's traffic receded from his ear, the smell of petrol from his nostrils and the sight of swarming humanity from his eyes. And the wide and gracious prospect of all Scotland (for so comprehensive was his imagination in exile)—the sight of all Scotland from the summit of the Pentlands filled not only his vision but his senses.

I chose the Pentlands for this nostalgic starting-point for my first book because they were familiar to me in my childhood, and the shapes and the heights and the roundnesses and the feel, and the very smell of the heather and the gorse and the bracken-scented air about them were amongst the first things I could remember. I still think, however, that to range along the tops of the Pentland Hills, whether one has been familiar with these hills in childhood or not, is to find about the best point in Scotland from which to look out over the country, from which to gather up in one armful of sight and imagined sight the various strands that go to weave the little kingdom of the north as it is today.

Southward there are the beginnings of the Border hills, which are all that lie between one and England. To the east the rich land of Lothian curves by the usually iron-grey North Sea and stretches by the Firth of Forth, in which are a variety of islands, not numerous, but precipitate, rocky, sturdy, highly individual, all of them, and each one a reminder that Scotland has more satellite islands within her domain than has any other country in Europe. To the west, Glasgow itself may be invisible, but the smoke within and around her does not so much hang upon the horizon as seem to murmur remotely and darkly in an echo of the innumerable sounds and activities of industrial Scotland. Below, under the protection of Arthur's Seat and Salisbury Crags, Edinburgh, too, wears her drifting crown of smoke, presenting from these heights and this distance an appearance that cannot have changed much over the centuries. And if the southern suburbs, with their little coloured bungalows, have crept up to the nearer foothills of the Pentlands, the sight of them does not affect one's view of the antiquity of the grey and ancient city; they are only a reminder of the continuity of time which, however it moves, will surely never touch that grey and massive profile of Castle, rocks and spires against the Firth of Forth, nor these hills upon which one is standing.

Then, with a lift of the heart as well as of the eyes, one looks northwards and north-westwards. There, beyond the immediate Ochils, are the first Highland peaks from Ben Ledi, Ben Vorlich to Ben Lomond. And if one has not been able to see Glasgow itself, it is something to be reassured by the sight of that famous mountain which, in the south-western thrust of the Highlands, has stepped down to the borders of Glasgow—that mountain above Loch Lomond which the Glaswegians have come to look upon as their very own. With that reflection there comes the thought that for the modern young Scot on his holiday, Scotland is no longer, as it once was, divided into two. At one time, and not so very far back in the past, the wall of the Highland hills represented a real and practical as well as a geographical dividing-line in Scotland.

Today, however, as the southern Scottish town-dweller out for a week-end climb or stroll amongst his own hills of home lifts his eyes to the distant Highlands he does not think of them as a wall within Scotland. Rather they appear to him as a prolongation of his own Scotland which he, the Lowlander or industrial worker, shares with the Highlander. The summits of Ben Ledi and Ben Vorlich against the northern summer sky, forty, fifty miles away, are a promise of delights which are as much his birthright as they are of any other Scot between the Mull of Galloway and John o' Groats, between Berwick and Cape Wrath.

They speak to him over the grey featureless belt of land that lies between the capitals of the East and of the West, over the Firth of Forth, over the Ochils, over the central plain of Scotland where centuries ago Scotland's freedom was fought for and won, over the Castle of Stirling itself. They speak to him of deeper, darker, lonelier, or more coloured hills and mountains of the north and the north-west, of the mountain lochs and lochans, of the Atlantic sea-lochs reaching deep into the heart of the country, of the silver sands of Morar, of the golden sands of Appin, of the pale-pink sands on the west of Coll and of the thousand and one islands and sea rocks of the Hebrides and the Norse Isles, all of which are as much a part of Scotland as are these Lothian hills upon which he now stands.

Hills is the operative word; for the face of Scotland is shaped and made and given its character by its hills. This is not to say that Scotland is, as Victorian and particularly as eighteenth-century Englishmen looked upon her, an unusually mountainous country. We have our mountains, of course, and some of them are famous not only amongst climbers but amongst lovers of scenery all over the world. The highest, however, Ben Nevis, is only 4,460 feet, which the average Swiss, French or Italian mountaineer might think of (in the words Dr. Johnson used when he wished to deflate Boswell's enthusiasm) as no more than "a considerable protuberance". We have, too, our wide valleys, our plains, our "carses" as they are known in the Scots tongue, but the very word carries an implication of a flat and fruitful place lying amongst hills which, though they may be upon the near horizon, are always visible. "I to the hills will lift mine eyes, from whence doth come mine aid"—so opens the 121st Psalm in the Metrical Version used in the Kirk of Scotland. They are words which have stamped themselves upon the mind and imagination of the Scot, even though he may not have been in church since he was a child. They have made their impression for the simple reason that wherever he has been in his native country he has always been able to lift his eyes to the hills. And whether he has found aid in them or not he has always found consolation; and the hills of his homeland are comforting as well as inspiring just because they are always there—in the best sense of the word, familiar.

This is brought home to the Scottish child or youth most forcibly when for the first time he goes into England. However much he may be excited by the novelty, pleased, moved and made comfortable by the unique beauty of the English countryside, its flatness, as compared with his native Scotland, takes him by surprise. The rich meadowland of the south, the villages that seem haphazardly to have grown out of the country itself cannot but enchant him when he first comes upon them, but after a while he comes to feel the lack of hills that used to be as much around him as the air itself, as much a part of the landscape as the very land on which he walked. And with that sense of something essential missing about him, there will be stirring in him the first hint of that homesickness for the soil, the land, the face of Scotland which, however far he may wander, may never leave him all his life.

A general hilliness begins immediately at the border between Scotland and England, and with it there goes an equally general austerity in the quality of the scene. This is partly due to the simple fact that Scotland lies to the north of England, but is more connected with the wrinkling of the earth's surface into hills. This is clearly demonstrated in that south-west and little-visited corner of Scotland, Galloway. Most of Galloway, which, as it were, hangs out of Scotland into the Irish Sea at the bottom left-hand corner, is well south of Northern England; and as it faces south-west and is protected by Ireland, its climate is balmy to the point of being relaxing. Not only do wild flowers and grasses grow there in its valleys in profusion, but there are also palms, which you will not find elsewhere in the British Isles until you get as far south as Devon and Cornwall. But there is a touch of austerity (albeit often a multi-coloured and romantic austerity) which at once proclaims that you are in Scotland. When, in high summer or on a forward spring day, you are standing in an unspoilt part of agricultural England, there is nothing on any side of you to break the view. You get the impression that the richness of the scene which is around you stretches not only to the horizon but for miles beyond, to the very sea itself where the island ends.

Not so in Galloway. Wherever you look there are hills and even mountains that interrupt the view, that remind you that, however industriously man may cultivate these protected plains and valleys, nature has abruptly and definitely set a limit to how far he can go. And though the contrast between fertile agricultural land and high, heather-covered or rocky hills is seldom anywhere else in Scotland so striking as in Galloway, it is a contrast that in varying degrees is cropping up with the hills nearly everywhere. If by carefully keeping away from the uplands and pressing into that other well-farmed part of Scotland in the north-east bulge south of the Moray Firth in Aberdeenshire you do manage to reach a place where the hills do not obviously protrude on the horizon, you will find another kind of austerity in the very air and colour of the Buchan scene which is quite as severe as anything produced by the ever-present hills.

The note of austerity, of wildness in the face of Scotland can, as the world has been reminded, perhaps too often, and too often with false sentiment, achieve romantic and beautiful effects. It can also chill the visitor and even depress the inhabitants when it becomes merely featureless and sour. There are parts of the central plain of Scotland, particularly the belt of land connecting Edinburgh and Glasgow, where one feels that even the outcrop of nineteenth-century industrialism in ugly little scars or strips cannot have done much to damage the original and natural dullness of the immediate landscape.

This austerity upon entering Scotland is discovered at its best at the north-east highway, either by road or by rail, by Berwick. The other two main and traditional land routes, by Carter Bar in the centre and by Carlisle and Gretna in the West, have their appeal, particularly Carter Bar with its fine prospect of the Borderland after the long climb from the deserted moors of Northumberland. To my mind, how-ever, the true drama of coming into or returning to Scotland is to be appreciated at its fullest by crossing the River Tweed at its mouth and by passing the Border-line three miles north, to the north of Tweed. It may be that memories stretching back deep into my own childhood have affected me—memories of the long journey up the full length of Eastern England, culminating at dusk or at dawn with the crossing of the historic river far below one, and, as one leaned out of the carriage window, of the faint sound of cheering and of the sight of hats and handkerchiefs being waved from other windows—but I think it is something more than childish recollection that has fixed my preference in this matter. Maybe there are racial memories in the

6　Looking south-east across the city of Dundee and the Firth of Tay

7   The River Dochart at Killin, Perthshire, with Ben Lawers in the background

8   The Bruar Falls near Blair Atholl, Perthshire

blood of any Scottish child which awaken at Berwick and come to life as he enters Scotland by this eastern route.

It was at Berwick and from this north-east corner of England that the blows of Edward I fell most fiercely upon Scotland. It has been said of the "Hammer of the Scots" that he did not so much break Scotland as hammer it into a fact. If so, that fact seems to have been most hardly and most obviously hammered out in Berwick-shire by the sea-coast where England has pressed upwards and northwards to squeeze the essence of Scotland into the texture, soil and appearance of this land, once so hardly fought over. It is not, I think, only fancy that makes it appear that history and geography have combined in this south-east corner of Scotland to proclaim the fact of Scotland to the incomer from the South.

As soon as the train has leapt high over the estuary of Tweed and passed through Berwick, a dramatic and, to a homecoming Scot, enlivening change takes place in the landscape, and indeed in the very seascape. The North Sea that now comes right up to the cliffland by which one is passing seems, as it dashes against the stones far below or eats into the land in narrow deep thrusts, wilder, greyer, less tamed than the more distant sight of it from the long plains of Northern England. The red soil of Eastern Scotland in the fields and in the strips of ploughland begins to show itself proudly like blood here and there in the closely farmed land that comes right to the cliff's edge. The hills begin at once to sweep up on the left, showing hints of the beginning of the Lammermuirs and to give promise of steeper, grander and remoter hills farther north and west—farther into the Kingdom.

The very architecture becomes suddenly, if not more austere, more firmly conscious of itself as built to withstand the north and the wild winds from the east. The farmhouses, sometimes whitewashed, sometimes grey, do not stand easily commanding their own land, but have sought shelter in clefts in the hillside, or if they do come out into the open and survey the world from a small hill-top, they do so with an air of defiance. Sometimes a previous generation has put a flimsy plantation around these exposed houses as a kind of gesture of protection. But, looking at them, Stevenson's lines recur to one:

> "A naked house, a naked moor,
> A shivering pool before the door,
> A garden bare of flowers and fruit
> And poplars at the garden foot:
> Such is the place that I live in,
> Bleak without and bare within.
> Yet shall your ragged moor receive
> The incomparable pomp of eve
> And the cold glories of the dawn
> Behind your shivering trees be drawn."

29

The very jingle of the familiar lines mingling with the beat of the train wheels as one is born northwards stimulates one with promises of home-coming. "Bleak without", maybe, but surely not so bare within. Here are thick-set walls and deep foundations; and even though the trees may shiver in the dawn there is warmth and protection against the fury of the north-east winds behind those same thick-set walls.

The train begins to leave the coast, the valleys inland begin to heighten and steepen, the little currents of water that tumble their way to the sea are no longer streams, they are burns. Now it is from the western side of the carriage that one begins to look, sometimes even lowering the window to try without avail to catch some hint of the inland steepness and remoteness that one knows awaits one farther on. Then the North Sea comes up again on the east side, and the ugly industrial patches (no more than patches) of East Lothian flash by amidst the richer farmland of one of the richest counties of Scotland. Then the ugliness of the industrial patches gives way to the even more forbidding grey disorder of suburban Edinburgh on the eastward side. It is a sight to chill the heart and yet at the same time to invigorate it with the shock of its chill. And then in a sudden, that chilliness gives way to a precipitous splendour. Arthur's Seat and Salisbury Crags, hanging over the railway and the petty train that runs along it, sweep all the suburbs aside in one commanding gesture. The train draws in under the glass roof of Waverley Station. You come out and climb the hill that leads you to Princes Street. It is still just light enough to see the mass of the Castle Rock, but the lights are beginning to come out from all over the heights and open spaces of this wide and precipitous city.

You are here again in the unchanging capital of Scotland. But you did not come into Scotland slowly, you came upon it miles back and in a sudden moment when, having passed the waters of Tweed, you entered the country by this the ancient north-east route, amidst the hills and uplands of Berwickshire and the Lothians. You came into Scotland by the austere route, the rocky route by the North Sea where centuries ago Scotland was hammered into herself: and the rocks and the sea and the hills and the soil itself seem still not to have forgotten it. Scotland began there.

9 Looking westward along the River Tay between Aberfeldy and Kenmore, Perthshire

II

I SEE my imaginary traveller as having come home to Scotland and to the capital of Scotland by this East Coast route and by rail. But, having stirred his middle-aged bones, and forced his flaccid leg muscles to carry him up to the highest point of the Pentlands above Edinburgh soon after his arrival, and having renewed this prospect of Scotland with which he was familiar in his youth, what, I ask myself, would he notice in the way of change over the years?

At first very little. The face of Scotland, both in its pleasing and in its less-pleasing qualities, is austere. Its bones are strong and near the surface: it cannot easily and quickly change its appearance. The wide prospect of the Lothians, the Firth of Forth, Fife, the industrial belt and of the distant Highlands is, from this high, commanding and traditional spot, much as it was twenty or thirty years ago. Perhaps it has changed little since R.L.S. himself climbed Caerketton, Allermuir and these other Pentland peaks above his own home of Swanston, which is still visible and unchanged down there amongst the trees. And the "T wood", which was for him, as for so many generations of Edinburgh schoolboys, *the* landmark of the Pentlands, is there as it always was, neither larger nor smaller, nor altered in outline by one foot; it seems as if it were a "petrified forest".

It is true that, as one looks down upon Edinburgh itself, one will notice here and there signs of this age. The suburbs have crept up to the very foothills and have blotted out the fields of Fairmilehead, which was once a real farm upon the edge of a capital city. As you came up through this new suburb you noticed the antennae of television masts sticking out from the roof of every second trim little building; and now from this height you can see the TV transmitting stations themselves on the nearby hills. There are other and larger and uglier suburbs stretching away out to the west which were not here even in 1939. The roads, or such of them as you can see, are more crowded with buses and motors—an incongruous "road house" actually shelters by Lothianburn—and there is a general air of increased movement and activity which is added to by the roar and whine of aircraft. On the whole, however, if you loved this prospect in youth, you need not fear a shock in coming upon it again.

As you look out over the wider and farther view, you may find it interesting to reflect that you are looking out not only over much of the land of Scotland but into her recent history. This recent history is not merely the story of what has happened in the last twenty or thirty years in this neighbourhood of Edinburgh, but is the story of how the appearance of Scotland has taken its present form over the last two centuries. From your viewpoint on these hills you can see the outward visible signs of much of these years that were so significant for Scotland.

Those rich lands of the Lothians below you and to the east are the product of the agricultural revolution which transformed the Lowlands of Scotland at the end of the eighteenth century. Before this revolution on the land, Scotland was, in farming, one of the most backward countries in all Europe. A pre-medieval and Celtic system of miserable strip-cultivation had lingered on right into Georgian times. And there was a touch of truth in the English eighteenth-century poet's jibe when he called Scotland "a land where half-starved spiders feed on half-starved flies". The peasants and small farmers who scratched a living from the soil were all but serfs; and it is small wonder that Scotland was then a land of soldiers, travellers, scholars, theologians—anything but cultivators of the soil. For in that pursuit lay only poverty that amounted to near slavery. All that was changed when Scotland adopted southern and scientific methods of farming a little under two hundred years ago. You can see the signs of that great and beneficent change in the lands of Lothian around the Pentland Hills today.

But there was another and even larger change which took place about the same time. The signs of this, too, you can see from the summit of the hills above Edinburgh when you look at the pall of smoke which hangs over Glasgow and the distant West. The agricultural revolution brought nothing but good to Scotland, but what of that other revolution that followed close upon it? What of that revolution which turned the pleasant, shallow, meandering little salmon river of the West into the clanging shipyard waterway of the Clyde, which burrowed beneath the belt of Central Scotland (through the gaping mouths of hundreds of pit-heads you can see the signs of some of them in the distance even from the Pentlands), which blackened more than one county with the smoke of its activity, which produced the cities of modern Glasgow and modern Dundee and half a hundred modern mining and industrial villages? This is a question that anyone who has looked out over the face of Scotland in the last hundred years, let alone today, may well have asked himself.

It is easy for those of us who have not earned our bread in such places, nor our own living out of the hard fact of industrial Scotland, those of us who love the width and freedom of the hills, and the untamed wildness of Scotland in her remoter parts, it is easy for us to turn away in distaste from the industrial revolution made by our Scottish forebears. And it is easy for my imaginary traveller and home-comer on the Pentlands and amongst the Lothian fields to share that distaste.

To turn away, however, from Scotland's industrial revolution is not only to try to avoid an inescapable fact but to neglect an important part of our heritage, of our achievement. In England, the industrial revolution was largely imposed upon the people of the country. In Scotland, for all its ugliness, it was a part of the people's national fulfilment. When, at the end of the eighteenth and in the early part of the nineteenth centuries, Scotland struggled for her place in the new world that was being born, she found means to her hand in the shipbuilding, in the iron-ore industry and in the coal beneath her surfaces. The new industry was a key which unlocked the door of wealth not only to a few men but to a whole country.

Small wonder then that the grim-faced descendants of the Covenanters, whose ancestors had struggled with the harsh lands of Scotland's miserable seventeenth- and early eighteenth-century farms, saw in this new development a struggle worthy of their powers and their belief. Small wonder that the more imaginative Celtic High-landers, driven by the circumstances of the time from their ancestral hills and coming in numbers into the industrial belt south of them, found something here in which they could combine their dreams and their frustrated powers of fighting. In Scotland, for all that it paid big dividends and was concerned with material things, the industrial revolution was a romantic national adventure.

The sense of adventure has passed; and much of the achievement of that adventure while it was new has gone with it. With the ending of the first world war and the withdrawal from Glasgow and the industrial West of the world markets, the great depression fell upon this part of Scotland—nor has it lifted yet. Something, however, of the romance remains. Glasgow is a town which is still fiercely loved, but is loved not only by Will Fyffe's "common auld workin' man" who under the glow of his Saturday night's whisky finds that he belongs to Glasgow and that Glasgow belongs to him. It is loved also with a peculiar concentration of affection, indeed a romantic affection, by all classes and conditions that call Glasgow their home.

There are only forty miles that separate Glasgow from Edinburgh, but they are forty miles that mark the difference between two worlds within the small country of Scotland. For this reason there is an odd sense of power, of excitement, in standing on the top of Edinburgh "hills of home" and being able to see from there the smoke above Glasgow and the West. This comes not only from the power of looking from one world into another, of spanning the whole width of Central Scotland with one's eyes, but from another reason also. No Scotsman with imagination could look upon that distant cloud without reflecting that under it there lies all that in the nineteenth century once made his country great, which still helps in a large measure to keep her great today.

The industrial revolution stained and scarred the face of Scotland with many blots, blemishes and wounds, but it also gave strength to the muscles of Scotland. And the character of Scotland as we know it today would not appear in her face if that revolution had not occurred as a part of our national fulfiment.

It was no accident that the large agricultural improvements and the industrial revolution occurred about the same time in Scotland. Before 1750 this country was one of the poorest in Europe; and "North Britain" had been, since 1707 and the Union of Parliaments, unquestionably the poor end of the island—so much so that in our modern speech it might have been called the "depressed area" of Britain. Politically, economically, and, some would have said, even spiritually, Scotland was moribund in the first half of the eighteenth century. In the 1730's grass was growing in summertime between the cobble-stones of the all-but-deserted High Street of Edinburgh; and this wild grass in the capital of Scotland has long been remembered as the outward sign of Scotland's depression and decay at her nadir. Then about half-way through the century something happened to free "North Britain" or the ancient Kingdom of Scotland. She stepped forward and with gusto to take her place amongst the countries of Europe. She reformed her agriculture, made Edinburgh a famous seat of learning (the "Athens of the North") and launched herself upon the adventure of industry. This something that happened was the passing of the old feudal Scotland and the coming of internal peace to a country which for two centuries had been almost uninterruptedly racked by civil dispute.

From the Pentland Hills you can see, on a fine day, almost the full length of the Highland line. You may reflect, as you look at it, that behind that line just before 1750 there began and ended a venture which marked the passing of the old Scotland, an event which left the way clear for the new country we know today. The failure of the last Jacobite rising in the Highlands in 1745–46 was not the primary cause of the industrial revolution and of Scotland's agricultural prosperity, but it was the "end of ane auld sang". And, above all, it was the beginning of internal peace, a peace which allowed men to go ahead in making the Scotland of the new world that began in the late eighteenth and nineteenth centuries.

The rising of '45 may have been the end of an old song, but it has been so celebrated in song and story since, that the last notes of the melodies it aroused have not been silenced yet. It has been much written about, continues to be written about, and can still in Scotland be the cause of popular and sentimental, as well as learned and historical, dispute. Whatever may be your political and historical views about it, however, you must recognize it as setting the stage for the Scotland of the improved Lowland farms and of the new industries. But what of the Highlands themselves, in which the last battle was fought out and where the old way of living in Scotland died?

Whether or not it was inevitable (and that is indeed a large question) the savage and thorough depopulation of the Highlands that followed upon Culloden was a national as well as Celtic disaster in Scotland. This is not the place to retell the sad old story of the economic failure of the Highlands from the latter half of the eighteenth century onwards, the impoverishment of the chiefs, the departure of the tacksmen, the eviction of the peasantry. Let it suffice to say that when you look at the Highland line from the distance above Edinburgh you are looking at a demarcation behind which, for a century and a half, lay that half of the land of Scotland once bitterly referred to as *Scotia deserta*.

Yet it is this *Scotia deserta* of which the average stranger to this country would think if anyone were to mention to him the phrase "the face of Scotland". In

10   Evening on Loch Insh near Kincraig, Inverness-shire

poetry, in pictorial art, in fiction, in legend, and even in music (such as Mendelssohn in his *Hebrides* or *Fingal's Cave* overture popularized a hundred years ago) the Romantic Movement presented the Highlands of Scotland to the world, and, as it were, sold the idea of Scotland to the world through this half, the deserted half of the country. Your stranger, your visitor to Scotland, if you were to set him down upon the place I have imagined upon the Pentland Hills, would not spend much time looking at and thinking about the Lowland farms of the Lothians or the industrial lands of the Clyde and West. His eyes would be leading him away from the top of the Pentlands, over the rocks of Edinburgh, across the Firth of Forth, away over the douce lands of Fife and over the central plains of Scotland to the distant line of the dark hills against the horizon. There, he knows, is the Highland line, and it is beyond and behind that line that he believes that he will find the true Scotland. Impatient for that "true Scotland" he would be ready, if anyone gave him the opportunity, to fly directly from these Lowland hills of the Pentlands into the heart of the Highlands of Scotland.

III

IT was with some reluctance that, for the first time, I agreed to fly by aeroplane over the Highland line and into the far north of Scotland. As a boy I had read in Walter Scott's *Rob Roy* Bailie Nicol Jarvie's unforgettable speech to the young visiting Englishman when he talked of the Highland line and the dark mystery that lay beyond it. It had made a deep impression on me; and even late into middle life I had never gone north into the hills without feeling that I was entering, re-entering perhaps for the hundredth time, a world different in kind rather than degree from the Lowlands of Scotland or from England, from the Saxon world in general where most of my working life had been and was being spent.

I knew, of course, that the world of Rob Roy had vanished before my great-grandfather had been born in the very Perthshire glens where Rob had lived. I knew that Gaelic had become a shy and all but secret language spoken by fewer and fewer people each year. I knew that modern transport and roads had brought the passes into the hills as near to Edinburgh as are the suburbs of Reading to London. I had, even as quite a young man, often breakfasted in Edinburgh or Glasgow, motored, or taken the train, into the Highlands, spent the day fishing or climbing, and had returned for supper. I knew all these things and had done all these things, but the Highland line had retained always something of its magic for me; and in the very desolation and deserted quality of even those Highland hills quite near to the large towns of the South I had felt the fact of another world at my own back door.

When, therefore, I had in middle life quite suddenly to fly from Glasgow over the Highlands to the Northern Atlantic islands of Shetland, I was a little fearful of the result. I knew that within five minutes of leaving the Renfrew airport I would see the first Highlands, and in ten minutes be over them. And then, I asked myself, what after that? Would the magic of the Highland approach be lost by this method, and be for ever after tarnished? And above all would my own massive Highland hills and mountains shrink into insignificance when I looked at them from above? Would what I had long thought of as grand and mysterious become, through this wretched bird's-eye view which I was compelled to take of it, merely petty and easily comprehensible? Would the Highland half of Scotland, would the grand prospect of *Scotia Deserta*, if you will, be rolled out below me as flatly as the marks on a map?

I need not have had any fears. I cannot say that I am fond of flying, and, when compelled to use the aeroplane in Europe, I have often felt a sense of disillusionment in passing so easily and quickly over seas, land and mountains, between London, Paris, Rome and the Greek Islands. But there was nothing of this in my first flight into the North of Scotland. There was no disillusionment but rather a shock of pleasant surprise in seeing from far above the abruptness of the Highland line. Even though we passed over it only a few minutes after leaving Glasgow and the Clyde, the fact that so large and so obvious a change could occur below one so soon and so impressively only emphasized the importance of it. There was no doubt about it: it was like flying out from the land over the sea.

Then, in a little, the Highland line was behind us, and I was plotting my way into the bulk of the Perthshire hills by the sight of the larger lochs and rivers that I knew and recognized below me. But in recognizing them I was surprised to find how many hill lochs and lesser peaks there were on this large landscape whose existence I had never dreamed of. How superficial, I now realized, had been my knowledge of even these Highlands so near to my home! I had wandered and climbed and fished over many of these hills. I was familiar with every hundred yards of every larger road through them, and had explored the more inaccessible passes on foot and on hill ponies in search of what I had believed were remote and hitherto unfished trout lochans. Only now, however, when I was ploughing my way through the clouds and the sky and the sunshine, did I understand that I had never before seen, let alone set foot on, one quarter of the wild and massive landscape below and around me, with which I had thought myself so familiar.

11 The monument to Bonnie Prince Charlie, Glenfinnan, at the head of Loch Shiel, Inverness-shire

12   Inverness: bridges over the River Ness from Castle Hill

13   In Glenshiel, Ross and Cromarty

A little later and we were over the great bulk of the Cairngorms. The long flat top of Ben Nevis, level with us on the left, showed through some strips of western cloud like the bottom of a huge upturned boat. Far away in the clearer north the fantastic shapes of the Sutherland peaks began to appear; and the Sutherland range itself as we approached it seemed to hang over the Caithness plain like a menacing wall. And now, exultant in this upper air, I realized that, for the first time in my life, I was seeing, looking at, almost comprehending the whole Highlands of Scotland in one grand compact mass.

It was for me an exhilarating experience, but one which made me resolve to be more than ever chary in the future of those glib generalizations which people make on the subject of "the Highlands". I had heard them talking about the Highlands as if they were merely some large district of Scotland which had become something of a problem, almost, as they would put it, a large "depressed area". Yes, I had actually heard that phrase used about the Highlands. And if, humanly speaking, there had not been a touch of bitter truth in it, there would have been something a little laughable in calling these great hills, stepping up one behind the other to the horizon, yet all of them together forming one comprehensive half of the whole face of Scotland, a "depressed area". Yet, as one looks at this same half of the face of Scotland from the air, one cannot but reflect that it was equally absurd to call it, as did our Victorian forebears, "the sportsman's paradise".

The Highlands of Scotland are amongst the oldest hills in the western world: beside them the Alps and the Pyrenees are *parvenus*. Before men ever came here, aeons before such problems as depressed areas or such pastimes as sport were even dreamed of by the most socially advanced cave-man, these hills were standing together in one great mass where now they are. And if circumstances around them have changed, and if Britain has become an island and no longer a part of the continent of Europe, and if the Atlantic has eaten into their western side in long sea-lochs, and if they have themselves become worn down in height in the passing of tens of thousands of years, their roots are still where they were when the Alps had not yet risen and the Thames was a tributary of the Rhine.

It is salutary to reflect on such things when one has the luck to look out over the whole Highland half of Scotland from the air and on a fine summer day. It is equally salutary to remind oneself of them when one is on the ground, whether one is looking at the distant line of the Highlands on the horizon from the Pentlands, or is discussing "the Highland problem" in the comfortable circumstances of an Edinburgh or Glasgow suburb.

A little over a thousand years ago the original Scots who founded the Kingdom of Scotland, and whom we now call the Gaels or Celts, began to inhabit and take over these immemorial uplands and islands of their new kingdom. A little under two hundred years ago, their traditional and feudal way of life having suffered defeat at

47

southern and Saxon hands, they were, decade after decade, driven from their ancient abodes. They were driven out sometimes by deliberate economic pressure, sometimes by happenings over which no one had any control and sometimes by eviction and brutal enforcement. A few of them remained, and they still preserve, amidst scenery as lovely as any to be found in Europe, their ancient language and their millennium of racial memories. What is to be the future of those who remain, and what is to be the future of the large vacant spaces of these ancient hills, valleys and moorlands made even more vacant and desolate by the departures of previous generations? That, in a few painfully compressed sentences, is the much discussed "Highland problem" of today.

Tempting though it may be for any Scot, particularly of Highland birth, to discuss the past, present and future of this problem, such a disquisition would have no place in this brief essay on the face of Scotland. It will be more profitable to consider what my imaginary traveller or homecomer on the Pentlands would find if he were to follow his inclinations and were to go north, not by air but on land, perhaps on foot, into the Highlands as they are today.

He would find that, as far as spectacular beauty of scenery goes, the Highlands have changed hardly at all over the years. Man has made remarkably little impression on these celebrated hills, either in his entry into them or in his enforced recession from them. In the old days it would indeed have been a heart-warming sight to have turned the corner by Kingshouse north of Strathyre and to have come across the populous Braes of Balquhidder under the Perthshire hills, and by the shores of Loch Voil. Today it is undoubtedly depressing to pass by the same shores and see only here and there the decaying stumps of what were once men's houses when Rob Roy lived and ruled in this region. But, as one lifts one's eyes to the hills above the now abandoned feet of the Braes, one is bound to admit that man has left little, if any, evidence either of his coming or his going upon these same hills. They stand here as they have stood for thousands of years; and for those of us who love their beauty they are as imperturbable as ever.

As he goes farther north, and even before he leaves the Perthshire Highlands, the traveller today will soon come across evidences of the new use that man is trying to make of these hills and their water-power. He will see the pylons striding across the moors and the hills. He will see modern buildings where men have dammed up the rivers. He will note where lochs have fallen many feet because of the water that has been drawn off; and he will hear tales of whole valleys that have been submerged to make new lochs in their place. But when he takes the wide view of all these changes and buildings that men have made in their harnessing of the ceaseless power of Highland water, he will be surprised to note how small they appear against the background of the great mass of even these Perthshire hills.

48

At one time we used to hear gloomy tales of how the amenities of the Highland scene were being threatened by the proposed hydro-electric scheme. If we hear no such complaints now it is not because people have grown indifferent to the amenities or accustomed to any hypothetical outrages against them, but simply because the Highlands (amenities or no amenities) have proved bigger than anything man can build upon them.

It is the same with the highways which, over the past two hundred years, advancing man has thrust into the Highland half of the face of Scotland. At one time General Wade's military roads seemed to threaten the whole north. Now these green ghosts of half-overgrown tracks, that waver this way and that through the glens and across the moors by the side of, and occasionally merging with, the more modern roads, have an almost pathetic look. It is not only that they are abandoned, given over to encroaching heather and bracken in favour of harder surfaces. They began to lose themselves long before that. The hills that they set out to conquer have conquered them.

In the reign of Queen Victoria, the romantics were upset at the notion of the railways penetrating the Highlands. It may have been partly for economic reasons; or it may have been that aesthetic objections also had something to do with it, but it is a fact that it was not until the middle 1890's that the railway line went beyond Fort William by Glenfinnan and Morar to Arisaig. Today that lovely stretch of country is still rightly looked upon as one of the brightest jewels in the crown of West Highland scenery. If one wanted to show the face of Scotland at its most beautiful, as well as at its wildest and best, to a visiting foreigner, one could not do better than to take him along the coast and amongst the hills from Glenfinnan through Morar. The thought of a railway line or a railway train being able to spoil such large perfection is almost laughable. Indeed, so far from spoiling it, the trains that puff their little way twice daily in and out amongst the huge foothills and across one enormous bridge seem only by their toy-like appearance to enhance the splendour of the scene.

It is the same even with the more menacing large road tracks along which every form of motor traffic can and does belch its petrol-laden way from the more populous southern districts daily. High-powered racing-cars, sixty-seater touring omnibuses from Blackpool with conductors shouting descriptions of the scenery through megaphones, and with portable lavatories in compartments behind the seating space, motor-cycles whose average speed is over one mile a minute, fleets of touring cars crowded side by side and bonnet to stern, lorries whose cargo sticks out on both sides to take up the whole road space and which rattle and bang and backfire so that they can be heard half a mile away—all these and other wheeled vehicles can pour along these great new roads between Perth and Inverness, between Glasgow and Oban, but the sum of their effect is eventually lost in the hills.

49

Difficult though this may be to believe, it is so. Anyone who doubts it may reassure himself by standing upon any high spot at the top of a glen and looking out over a number of miles of Highland scenery through which one of the main roads passes. He may choose as fine a day as he pleases in high summer, and when the traffic is most congested and at its noisiest. It may take him some time to reach his point of vantage from the main road, perhaps half an hour, but he will be rewarded.

When he turns to survey the scene below him, and far away from him and from which he has walked, he cannot but observe how astonishingly insignificant the road and its burden will have become. Within half a mile's distance the road will have shrunk to the thinness of a piece of desiccated tape, lost amongst the width of moorlands, and overhung by the height of hills which, however far back he may step to look at them, still keep their great size. The traffic, if not actually invisible, seems in the distance to be no more than a procession of slowly moving small insects. And how soon that procession loses itself as it moves away!

The pylons, the new buildings to shelter the electric generators, the houses that have sprung up around them, the railways, the little railway stations, even the full length of all the hard-surfaced main roads that stretch from one end of the Highlands to the other—add them all together and they do not take up more than one-thousandth part of the surface of this part of the face of Scotland. And when you think of that surface as being broken by great heights, deep valleys, wide forests of plantations, and washed by quickly rising and tumbling rivers, the insignificance of that thousandth part on which man has made his mark becomes even more trivial and more easily forgotten.

If the traveller of whom I am thinking has not crossed the Highland line for thirty years or more he need not fear that the "march of progress" will have done much to damage a scene which has withstood not only centuries but millennia. If he is observant, however, he may notice one change that has taken place since his youth. It is a change as much in the human atmosphere of the Highlands of today as in their physical aspect. This change can best be summed up by saying that the Highlands are now, for the most part, open to the people of Scotland.

In the distant past, over two hundred years ago, this was true to the extent that the people, or at least a large number of the Celtic peoples of Scotland, were able to live amongst their traditional hills, and in the glens and valleys which their fore-fathers had inhabited before them. When these Highlanders at the end of the eigh-teenth and the beginning of the nineteenth centuries were expelled and their places were taken by sheep and deer, it would perhaps be too much to say that the High-lands became, for human visitors, a forbidden territory. It is true, however, that in the century of the great sporting proprietors, man was made to feel unwelcome on this part of the face of Scotland. In entering the Highlands, the walker, the cyclist, the humble tourist was a creature very much on sufferance. He was fearful of leaving

14 Looking to Bidean nan Bian in the mountains above Glen Etive, Argyllshire

15　The ruins of Dunnottar Castle, south of Stonehaven, Kincardineshire

16   Looking across Gruinard Bay to the distant peak of Ben More, Coigach, Ross and Cromarty

the roads in case he "disturbed the game". Though in law much of the moving water was actually free to him, if he carried anything that looked like a fishing rod he was an object of suspicion to any roving gamekeeper. He was forbidden to camp. And even the traditional hospitality of the Highlands was often denied to him by crofters who feared to offend their landlords by "taking in tourists".

Today many of the great estates have crumbled and gone, or been split up. It is as yet uncertain what will take their places—the new buildings of the hydro-electric scheme, new farms; or perhaps here and there those ardent young spirits from the towns, the young men who wish to return to the land and take over abandoned crofts, may even make and leave their mark. But in general the passing of the large old preserves has left space which has, as yet, not been practically occupied. The young people, the young hikers, tourists, cyclists, campers from the towns of the South have become aware of this freeing of the land north of the Highland line, and they have not been slow to take advantage of it.

From early spring till that late autumn which, in these northern parts lingers on until November, you can see the weekly, the daily trek of young and middle-aged people who are entering the Highlands for the first time to enjoy them as a part of their heritage. These new incomers to the Highlands do not by any means always stick to the roads. They climb the mountains, use forgotten hill passes, camp by the shores of hill lochans, and fish for their breakfast in the water of the same lochans. Sometimes they walk, sometimes cycle, and, of recent years, have taken to hiring hill ponies on which they ride about in droves. On the whole, they are welcome to the Highlanders who live all the year round in these districts. They do very little harm, and bring life and youth and a sense of adventure into these wild and recently abandoned parts.

Perhaps one or two of them may make a nuisance of themselves by getting lost on a mountaineering expedition and having to be rescued. Perhaps one or two of them are a little over-free with what they consider to be their right over the trout waters. Perhaps they are sometimes noisy. But how small are these lapses when considered against the large background of the Highland scene! The opening of the Highland part of Scotland to the people of Scotland has been the greatest change that has happened in these hills in the last thirty years. With all its minor drawbacks, it is a change which only the most selfish and stony-hearted lover of solitude could deplore.

These young people have turned for their freedom to the hills and the Highland parts of their native land. And in doing so they have turned not to the most accessible and easy but to the most famous parts long celebrated in history, romance and legend.

This is not because these young people are in the least under the influence of what used to be known as the "Romantic Movement", still less by the later

57

Victorian backwash from that movement. They would probably be bored by Walter Scott's descriptive prose on Highland scenery, and would consider his romantic verse to be jingle. They would be frankly, and rightly, repelled by Scott's imitators. They go to the Highlands of Scotland simply because these Highlands are free and wide and open to them, and because they find such scenery beautiful.

In this surely they are right. The Highland parts of Scotland have been the subject of much sentimental, meretricious and third-rate art; but it would be a mistake to allow oneself to be put off by this. It would be a mistake not to recognize the fact that the Highland view of Scotland caught our Victorian grandfathers' and great-grandfathers' imagination by qualities which were unique in Britain, are still unique, and which are rare, some would say unique, in all Europe.

Unique is a strong word, but it can be used about the unsullied beauty of certain parts of Scotland. There are, as has already been said in this essay, hills and ranges on the continent of Europe that are higher, twice as high as the highest of the Scottish Highlands; there are mountain formations that are more massive, peaks that are more difficult to climb, and, in Scandinavia, hills and mountains more remote. But nowhere else in Europe than in the ultimate West Highlands will you find a combination of remoteness and grandeur with such a profusion of what I hope it is not sentimental to describe as tender beauty.

The lover of the face of Scotland can point to many and varied scenes which delight the eye and tug at the heart of the homecomer. Your Borderer may feel, as he crosses the line between England and Scotland, that these the southern hills of his land with their long history behind them, their rich farmlands enclosed in them, Tweed running through them, are all that he would wish for on his return; and he may not be tempted farther north. The Fifer or the Aberdeenshire man may feel, understandably, that the essential Scotland shows itself in the beautiful austerities of the sea coast and inland plains between Forth and Moray. Your Perthshire man may praise the Rob Roy country, your Gallowegian may feel that in his undisturbed south-west corner of Scotland he has the best of both worlds, Highland and Lowland. Put any of these, however, or indeed any Scot, down upon the north-west seaboard upon a fine June day or during one of our long autumnal spells of golden undisturbed weather, and for sheer spectacular beauty of scene he will have to admit defeat.

The young people who nowadays flock into the Highlands and, at the end of their journey, make their way to these regions of the West would hesitate to put such thoughts into such words. Nevertheless, I cannot but feel that in turning instinctively north and west to this part of the face of Scotland they are turning to what they recognize in their hearts to be the loveliest and best part of it—now at last open to them.

17   In the Kintail Hills at the head of Loch Duich, Ross and Cromarty

IV

SCOTLAND, as has often been pointed out, is a country of extremes and of contrasts; and contrast is frequently shown in the look of Scotland. It would be difficult, however, even in this diverse land, to choose a greater contrast than that between the West Highlands and the North-East Lowlands. It is a contrast not of hill and plain, of cultivated land and of bare upland, of population and desolation, of farmland and moor, of a land of the immemorial past and of the solid present (though all these elements do enter into the differences between, say, Wester Ross and Buchan) but of the very soil, rocks, sea and air itself. From the north part of the face of Scotland down to the south there runs a wavering line which not only separates the west of the country from the east, but which seems to mark a split in the quality of the earth's surface and of the atmosphere about that surface.

The western side of Scotland is mountainous and grand to the eye, but its core is soft. It is the easy prey of the wind and the waves. One glance at the map will suffice to show this. You will see how in the centuries the Atlantic and the west winds have torn off, from the mountain masses, ridges and ranges, nearly a thousand islands and isolated rocks which are now scattered far out to sea. You will see where the fingers of salt water which not so very long ago began to feel their way about the crevices of the coast and which are now long arms thrust into the very heart of the hills. They make those sea-lochs which, though they add so notably to the beauty of the West Highland scene, are a confession of the West Highlands' failure to withstand the elements.

On the east, that uncompromising hump of Scotland between the River Tay and the Moray Firth faces with an imperturbable challenge the far more savage onslaught of the weather that comes down from Scandinavia and from the Russian steppes. Here are no flourishing mountain tops, no jagged skylines, no "awe-inspiring" relics of the ceaseless battle between sea and land—only the hard solid fact of the victory of the land in this particular part of Scotland. The soil and rock of Aberdeenshire, of Angus, and even of the little "Kingdom of Fife", have no need to show by fretted coast-line, by isolated mountains, and by challenging cliffs, that they are conducting a struggle far more arduous than that which the West Highlands have had to endure; they simply sit there in the teeth of the wind and the waves, presenting a contour of landscape and coastline that remains unmoved, unruffled and undisturbed.

This difference is reflected in the atmosphere of the West and the East. The West is relaxing. Soft rains, soft mist and occasional days of soft, long luminous sunshine add to the beauty of the West Highland scene. They also express in the very air itself the softness of the changing and malleable earth beneath. In the East, even upon the very finest day of a late summer, you are always conscious of the whip-crack of the north-east just round the corner. You must always be ready to endure not only the buffet of storm but the sting of wind and icy rain. And, if ever you are tempted to give in, to retreat before them, you must take heart, as well as you can, from this intractable landscape around you which unmoved has withstood thousands upon thousands of years of such weather before you ever came here, and will withstand thousands more after you are gone, without allowing this part of the face of Scotland to change one whit.

Lest it seem that I am painting a picture of some rocky north-eastern howling wilderness of desolation, let me hasten to say that in this uncomfortable hump of Scotland there lie the lands of Aberdeen, Buchan, the Mearns and Angus, and that there is no finer farming country in all Scotland, nor is there anywhere in the country where the land is better farmed. The soil is rich, well watered by rivers and streams that flow evenly all the year round and do not rise and fall and tumble and break their banks as in the West. If it is open to the harsh winds from the north-east, it is protected by the mountain ranges to the west and the south; and those very winds serve to keep the soil within this saucer of land evenly distributed over a rocky foundation which stands deep, fair and square, resolute against the worst that the sea can do to undermine it.

The people that farm this part of Scotland, that live in its towns and villages, are as different from their fellow-countrymen in the West as are their landscape and their weather from those of the Atlantic seaboard. They are hard workers, not very imaginative, not easily depressed or put down, dogged in defence of their land and their habits, and not given to a desire to extend the frontiers of that land or to travel. Just as this hump of Scotland forms a hard, solid, immovable and unchanging entity in and on the face of Scotland, so do these North-Easterners form a kind of hard core of Lowland Scottishness, not so much in the heart of the Lowlands as on their sea frontiers. Their speech is unaffectedly unselfconsciously Scottish. They do not look upon it as a dialect, but, with some justification, as a language, a form of Scots or, if you will, English which has its unquestioned and unassailable place in the variety of tongues spoken in the British Isles.

It would be unjust to speak of their admirable self-sufficiency as self-satisfaction, but they undoubtedly incline to believe that they and their north-east country represent not only the heart of Scotland, the true Scotland, but sometimes all of Scotland that matters. There is a saying in the grey granite capital of this hump of the Lowlands, "Tak awa' Aiberdeen an' twal mile roon and faur are ye?" This, even

62

the most fervent Aberdonian patriot would admit, is a trifle restrictive, and, if you pressed him, he would extend his "twal mile roon" to take in a larger area. But the true meaning of the saying is "Take away Aberdeen and the North-East and what remains of Scotland?—nothing."

From this it may be judged that the North-East folk of Scotland are, on the whole, content with their lot and with their land. If their own solid virtues and their industrious cultivation of their bleakly exposed, but fundamentally rich, soil has had much to do with this they have also been helped in their contentment by the fact that the years have brought singularly little change to this part of Scotland. This is not to say that the North-East lives in anything of a backwater. Economically, Aberdeen and the country round it have survived two world wars with little damage just because Aberdeen and the North-East have kept on doing their job unperturbed by the rage of outside events.

Something of this highly business-like conservatism, which keeps the past living on in the most practical and unsentimental manner in the present, shows itself in the outward aspect of the north-east face of Scotland. Aberdeen granite is one of the most durable of stones in the world; it is also superficially one of those least subject to change. Two houses in Aberdeenshire, standing side by side, may have been built the one a hundred years or more later than the other, but it will be difficult to tell from the outside which is the older and which is the newer house. There are certain streets and crescent squares in Aberdeen put up under the graceful influence of late Georgian or Regency architectural fashion a hundred and fifty years ago. Yet so fresh and clean and utterly unaltered are their façades that it is difficult, when looking at them, not to believe that some modern architect and some builder of the 1950's have not amused themselves by erecting a deliberate pastiche in the old manner and with old drawings to guide them.

It is the same in the country towns and villages, and even in the countryside of the North-East. It is remarkably difficult to tell at first how old or how new a building, a farmhouse, or even a whole township, may be. The last two hundred years in this part of Scotland have not grown and changed and decayed or mellowed; they have simply and obstinately remained a part of the present.

The far North-East of this hump of Scotland, the land of Buchan, is seldom visited by tourists to Scotland. If it is admirable farming land, and if there are many creature comforts to be found in it, its aspect is bleak, and its weather can be punishingly cruel. For those who have got to know it, however, as well as for those who have been born and brought up in it, it has its appeal. Its grey horizons and skies, its dark green grassland, its rocky coasts, its dark red soil when under the plough give it a kind of austere majesty. On the one side of it is the grey North Sea. In the distance there are the inland hills; but between them it stands there one of the most indestructible and least changing parts of all Scotland; and as such it is loved by its children:

> "This is my country,
> The land that begat me.
> These windy spaces
> Are surely my own.
> And those who here toil
> In the sweat of their faces
> Are flesh of my flesh,
> And bone of my bone.
>
>   *   *   *
>
> Yet do thy children
> Honour and love thee.
> Harsh is thy schooling,
> Yet great is the gain:
> True hearts and strong limbs,
> The beauty of faces,
> Kissed by the wind
> And caressed by the rain."

The well-known poem from which this is a quotation was entitled by its author, Sir Alexander Gray, "Scotland", and no doubt he had the whole country in mind when he composed it. These two stanzas, however, which I have printed above, have seemed to me to contain the essence of the appeal of the far North-East. "Bone of my bone", the poet has said. The North-East is the very bone of the face of Scotland, but in its austerity, as well as in its unchanging indestructibility, it is none the less beautiful for that.

The North-East shades down in its severity as it comes south. And though the Berwickshire and Lothian lands, which I have already spoken of in my first chapter, may seem austere enough to the traveller coming into Scotland by the eastern route, they would certainly not seem austere to the Aberdeenshire man on his way south. But before he came to the Lothians he would have to pass another and highly self-contained unit of this same eastern part of Scotland—Fife.

Fife, lying as it does between the estuaries of the Firth of Tay and the Firth of Forth, is nearly three parts an island. It is highly conscious of its individuality; and the more old-fashioned people when writing of it still sometimes call it "the Kingdom of Fife". Despite its nearly isolated position, it is very much a part of the chain of hard, obdurate land that goes to make up the east of Scotland, and is a link that connects the rich land of the Lothians with the lands (rich in a different kind) of Buchan and with even that remote outpost of the North-East, Caithness.

64

18   The Brig o' Dee, near Braemar, Aberdeenshire

Part of Fife is farmland, part of it, in the west, is increasingly given over to mining and to industry; and a distinct part of it draws its livelihood from entertaining visitors to Scotland and from other parts of Scotland, who love the austerities, beauties and holiday facilities of Scotland's East for their own sake, and precisely because they offer such a contrast to the more celebrated Highlands and the West. It is not only the fact that the most famous golf course in the world is at St. Andrews in Fife, and that there are other celebrated courses in the neighbourhood that draw these holiday crowds. East Fife, with its rocky coast, its grey sea, its old fishing villages and its quiet sense of history pervading everything, has its lovers who would smile at the notion that it is in the Highlands and in the more "extrovert" West that you will find the true face of Scotland.

As has surely already been made abundantly clear, there is no one part of Scotland's surface that truly represents the quality of all Scotland—though Galloway makes a spirited attempt to combine as many qualities as it can. In Fife, however, you will find a microcosm of nearly all the qualities of Scotland's eastern and bony skeleton. It was in the East of Scotland that most of the country's history since the early Middle Ages has been decided. Fife has provided the stage for much of that history to be enacted; and the feel of that past history haunts all East Fife. The East of Scotland has provided the best farming tradition since the agricultural revolution; and Fife still contains farmland that withstands all the attempts from the west to industrialize the county. The East of Scotland is the home of the North Sea fisheries, and Fife's coast is dotted with fishing villages and ports from which boats trade with all Britain and with Europe. Finally, the Fifer, with his long, dry, humorous visage, if usually unsmiling expression, his dry laconic wit, and his mastery of understatement, has become for many visitors to Scotland the type *par excellence* of the East Coast Lowlander, and as such is often taken (though wrongly) as being the pure essential Scottish "character".

No chapter devoted to that long hard ledge of land which protects the north end of the island of Britain from the fury of the north-east seas and winds would be complete without a mention of the often neglected county of Caithness.

Those who have never been to Scotland sometimes think of this extreme north-east tip of the country, beyond the hump of Buchan, beyond the Moray Firth, and beyond the hills of Ross-shire, as being part of the North Highlands of Scotland. Nothing could be further from the truth: there is no flatter piece of ground in all Scotland than that triangle which lies between the Sutherland mountains and the North Sea with Norway beyond. Indeed, even in all Britain, East Anglia included, it would be difficult to find a more level piece of British soil.

Caithness used at one time to be known as the granary of the kings of Norway. And, in the days when the Scandinavians were still disputing parts of the mainland of Scotland with the Scots, this flat and comparatively rich piece of remote soil used to provide the Vikings with a better place for the cultivation of their crops than any that they could find amongst their own mountainous and fiord-fretted country. It is many centuries since the last long black Viking ship left the shores of Caithness for home, laden with agricultural produce to help the Norwegians across the sea to outlast their winter. Nevertheless there is still in the atmosphere of Caithness an air faintly foreign to the rest of Scotland.

The foreign atmosphere may be partly due to the flatness of nearly the whole shire. This flatness comes upon the traveller to the north with all the greater shock because he has everywhere else in the more southern parts of Scotland grown so accustomed to hills and thinks of them as an inevitable part of the Scottish and northern scene. The foreign atmosphere is also undoubtedly partly due to the extreme northern light which in summer time seems to stream endlessly over these wide horizons in an unfamiliar and un-British way.

There is also a faintly foreign air to be observed amongst the folk of Caithness. There is more than a strong dash of Scandinavian blood in them. Yet they have for centuries farmed their lands and gone from their fishing-ports always conscious that they have lain under the shadow of some of the largest and certainly the most fantastically shaped peaks in all the Highlands of Scotland—the Sutherland Hills. There is no touch of Gaelic in the Caithness speech, and there can be in them only a small admixture of Celtic blood, nevertheless it is perhaps not too fanciful to suppose that the presence, the looming presence, of the great hills on their immediate west has affected their character. The Caithness man, like his strangely beautiful county, is undoubtedly a product of Eastern Scotland, but he is in certain essentials a man apart. And Caithness itself, flat, rich in farmland in parts, covered by moors in others, based on immovable rock, displays many of the physical characteristics of the long ridge of Eastern Scotland. At the same time, separated as it is by mountains and by Firths from the other parts of that ridge, it is something of an island on the far north edge of the mainland of Scotland.

I do not know whether anyone, apart from surveyors, lighthouse inspectors or men interested in fisheries, has attempted a conspectus of the whole eastern ridge of Scotland. It has sometimes occurred to me, however, that a long slow tour from Berwick to John o' Groats would provide an original holiday for someone interested in the not too obvious parts of the face of Scotland. In making such a journey, one would be conscious all the time of going along a well-defined but often interrupted path. Arms of the sea, towns, industrial and mining districts would here and there get in the way of one's progress, but if one held one's course one would be rewarded in the end. The eastern side of Scotland has been the bulwark of the country against more than the North Sea and the north wind. It has contributed to, as well as strengthened and protected, the character of Scotland. It would be interesting to explore this part of Scotland from end to end.

68

19   St. Andrews from the Golf Links

20   Looking to Slioch from the fringes of Loch Maree, near the Bridge of Grudie, Ross and Cromarty

21   The Abbey, Dunfermline, Fife

V

THE more perfervid Scot has been known to envy Ireland the fact that she is entirely surrounded by water. He may console himself, however, by reflecting that, if his own country so narrowly, and by so short a strip of land, misses being an island, she does at least possess more islands off her coasts than does any other country in Europe. There are seven hundred and eighty-seven officially listed "Scottish islands"; but if we add to this number the many quite sizeable pieces of barren land and large rock formations in the sea, uninhabited by men or sheep or any domestic animals, there are over two thousand. Most people are unaware of this impressive figure—and, furthermore, it is safe to say that there can never have been anyone who has set foot on every Scottish island.

I state this categorically because, quite apart from the extreme improbability of anyone having had the time to visit all the islands in the Inner and Outer Hebrides, in Shetland, in Orkney and in the North Sea, it is known that no one has ever been able to put ashore on that remotest piece of Scottish land, Rockall. It is, incidentally, interesting to reflect that, should two people succeed in getting on to this desolate and precipitate mass of rock over two hundred and fifty miles out into the Atlantic ("the most isolated speck in the world") and should one of them push the other over the seventy-foot cliffs he would, if captured, be tried by Scottish law, before a jury of fifteen, and might escape on a verdict of not proven.

The two thousand or so islands off the Scottish coasts are not only obvious and important geographical facts, they have played an important part in Scottish history. It has been to the islands that defeated men and defeated races have retreated for security; at the same time it has been from the islands that new blood has come into the Scottish life-stream through invasion. The Celts may have largely lost their battle for survival as a race on the mainland of Scotland, but they have fought a notable rearguard action in the islands. The result has been that you will find in the Outer Hebrides the only true and satisfactory survival of the pure Gaelic way of life in Scotland, and the purest and strongest living Gaelic language. On the other hand, there has been a flow from these islands on to the mainland in reverse. It was from these same islands that there has come into the body of Scotland the strong strain of Scandinavian blood in our veins, as a result of the Viking conquest of the Hebrides, and the original Viking possession of Orkney and Shetland.

Today the islands are unlikely to act as a source for any new influence into the blood-stream of Scotland. Nevertheless, they play their part in preserving locally the purity of part of that blood-stream and from time to time re-injecting that purity into the main body. Gaelic culture, and possibly even the Gaelic language, would have been almost extinguished by now if it had not been for the island population of the West. In the far north, too, the Orcadians and the Shetlanders may have lost the old Norse tongue in its purity, but, as any visitor to their archipelagos soon finds out, they most certainly have not lost their Norse affiliations. People in the main body of Scotland are frequently reminded of the part that the Norsemen have played in their history, not only by looking at the map and glancing at the district islands in the North Atlantic, but by the arrival in their midst of their own Norse compatriots (Norse in blood, culture and attitude of mind, but Scottish by law and custom) from Orkney and Shetland.

It is through the map, however, that the islands make their first and often lasting impression on the minds of most Scottish people. There can be few Scottish children whose imagination now and again has not been stirred by the sight of the scattered archipelagos which they see marked on the large maps of their country, hanging on their schoolroom walls. Perhaps they have tried to count the islands and have failed, perhaps they have amused themselves by noting the strange names that some of them possess—Rum, Eigg, Muck, Yell, Papa Stour and so on, but surely their childish fancy must at one time or another have led them on imaginary voyages amongst these, to them, innumerable parts of the body of Scotland scattered in the sea around their country.

Up to the present such imaginary journeys are, it must be admitted, about as much travelling as most Scots manage to achieve amongst the distant isles. Most native Scots at some time have been to one or more of the nearer holiday isles off the West Coast and in the Firth of Clyde; and there can be very few of even the most stay-at-home people in Scotland who have not seen some of our islands from off the mainland, but that is all. They are conscious of the islands, they are aware of the influence the islands have had and still, to a certain extent, have upon us, and they may take a kind of pride, as it were, in the romantic fact of the islands, but they seldom visit them.

On the other hand, the native islanders are now, as never before, constantly visiting the mainland and easily returning to their own islands. The reason for this is modern air traffic, which has undoubtedly had a beneficial effect on island life in general. The aeroplane allows the remotest Hebridean or Shetlander to visit Edinburgh, Glasgow or Aberdeen, and return home on the next, or sometimes even on the same day. He feels, therefore, that he can keep in personal touch with life in the main centres of Scotland without having to uproot himself from his island. It may be that, when air traffic becomes even more general, the flow will also set in in the other direction, and that the ordinary mainland Scot will get into the habit of visiting the islands as he now visits and enjoys the Highlands and the open hillsides near to his own home.

No one who knows and loves the islands, and who approves of the tendency which I have already mentioned for the young people of Scotland to explore and to enjoy their own heritage of the remoter parts of their own country, could regret the inclusion of the islands in that heritage. For too long have the islands been drained of human life, for too long have they been regarded as lonely outposts, becoming more and more lonely each year. If the aeroplane can help to keep the indigenous islander at home, it can also help to keep the islands truly a part of Scotland. It can help them to live in the stream of the life of Scotland of today, because Scottish people from the mainland will be coming to them and visiting them and enjoying them as part of their heritage.

And what a rich new part of that heritage will now be opened up to these new visitors to the islands! There is first of all the appeal of variety. In the broad field of choice there are four distinct archipelagos with four distinct different characteristics to choose from—Shetland, Orkney, the Inner Hebrides and the Outer Hebrides.

Shetland is the least known of the Scottish group of islands, and, until recently, was but rarely visited save by anglers, bird-watchers and lovers of the extreme north. The aeroplane has now brought Sumburgh Head in Shetland within two hours' flying distance of the south of Scotland, and every year more and more people are going to these ultimate islands to enjoy "the Simmer dim" (the romantic Shetland phrase for the light that lasts all through the short Shetland midsummer night), the rocky coasts, the delicate colouring, the wildness, the sense of remoteness and "foreignness" which are to be found in these, the most northerly part of the British Isles.

Orkney is just as obviously, and, as far as the inhabitants are concerned, just as consciously Norse as is Shetland, but in a less spectacular way. The Shetlander is a fisherman or sailor who has a croft; the Orcadian is a crofter or farmer who has a boat. Something of the difference between these two groups of islands can be seen on the map. Shetland is an attenuated strip of scattered rocky islands that look as if they had been thrown out in a kind of "slip-stream" from the main body of Scotland far into the North Atlantic. Orkney is a round group of islands sitting comfortably together just off the flatly and evenly cut north coast of Scotland.

Shetland is rocky and precipitate: Orkney is flat, covered with good soil, and is one of the best farming counties in all Scotland. The Shetlander's Norse blood leads him to sail the seven seas. The same blood in the veins of the Orcadian makes him struggle with equal ardour with his land. He stays at home; and home, in his instance, means not Scotland or Great Britain, or other Norse lands, but his own closely knit group of islands. His excellent farming, and his capacity for sticking to the land, had made him a prosperous man, but it has not led him to travel. Just

77

before the war there were still well-off farmers on Orkney who possessed motor-cars and who used the island air service to travel by aeroplane between the different islands of Orkney, but who had never seen a railway train—for they had never been on the mainland of Britain.

There is beauty of an austere and remote kind in these two groups of islands off the north of Scotland; but it is in the Hebrides, both Inner and Outer, that the true loveliness of Scottish island scenery is to be enjoyed at its best. The Hebrides are really an extension of the West Highlands into the Atlantic, and they carry with them out to sea the beauty of that celebrated mountain group and coast-line. The Hebrides can be as remote as the Norse islands, and can present as forcibly as they do the appearance of having been forgotten by the world, but they have nothing of the grey harshness of the north about them. They are multi-coloured and can change their colours many times in one day with the changing weather, but this colour is never garish, never crude, always soft and appealing, however rich and varied it may be.

Most Scots people have some idea of the appearance of the better known of the Inner Hebrides, and many of them have visited one or two of them. Something, but only something, of the precipitous grandeur and fantastic beauty of the most famous of all the Hebrides, Skye, has been made familiar to us by many pictures and even by railway posters. And Skye is visited each year by thousands of tourists and holiday-makers, not only from Scotland but from all over the world. The islands of the Clyde estuary, and in particular Arran, are even better known than Skye to the ordinary Scots folk. It is nearly a century now since the people of the expanding city of Glasgow began to make use of the beauties that lay by water immediately at their own back door. And if the beauties of Arran have become familiar to many generations of holiday-makers, that familiarity has certainly not bred contempt. Arran, for all the crowds that go to it every year, retains not only its beauty but its grandeur as one of the most impressive as well as the loveliest of all Scottish islands.

But there are a hundred or more of the Inner Hebrides, lying not far off the Scottish coast, which are unexplored and seldom visited. Iona is, of course, famous, partly for its beauty and partly for its great history; but what of Coll, Eigg, Muck, Colonsay, Raasay, Gigha, to name only a few of the smaller islands whose names come immediately to mind, islands which are each of them individually as lovely as any of the more celebrated Inner Hebrides? And, above all, what of the grandeur and beauty of the all but desolate island of Rum on which no one nowadays is allowed to land? There is a wealth of beauty and variety awaiting exploration and enjoyment—waiting just off the coasts of Western Scotland.

The Outer Hebrides, comprising that long strip of islands from Lewis to Barra Head, are even less visited than are the smaller of the Inner Hebrides, but their fame has travelled farther. The "Songs of the Hebrides", which Mrs. Kennedy

22   Loch Coruisk and the Cuillin Hills, Isle of Skye

23   Balmoral Castle and the mountains of Balmoral Forest, Aberdeenshire

24 The harbour, Aberdeen

25   The harbour at Crail, Fife

26 Barcaldine Castle and Loch Creran, Argyllshire

Fraser collected and popularized at the beginning of this century, made the names of Eriskay and Barra well known not only in Scotland but all over the world. The revival of interest in the Gaelic language and in Gaelic culture has in the last twenty years drawn attention to these islands, where the purest Gaelic does something more than "still survive".

The Outer Hebrides are less spectacularly beautiful than the more celebrated of the inner group, but their remoteness and the quiet delicacy of their colouring have an appeal which it is difficult to resist. Air traffic is already making this, the most western part of the body of Scotland, more accessible; and there are lovers of the "farthest Hebrides" who return there every year to enjoy a kind of island life which a few years ago had been all but forgotten by this century.

The islands of Scotland (save on the map, where they always cut a romantic and attractive figure) have long been a half-forgotten part of the face of Scotland. Of recent years they had not only been forgotten but were, humanly speaking, dying. They had always been cut off, but within the last half-century life was increasingly draining away from them. Is it too much to hope that the new feeling which the people of Scotland are beginning to develop for the land of Scotland, combined with the new facilities for travel, may stem this tendency? Is it too much to hope that the indigenous island life may be preserved by ameliorating the lot of the native islander, and that new life as well may be brought to the islands by the people of Scotland, who will come to know their lovely archipelagos as something more than attractive and romantic marks on the map?

The Hebrides are celebrated in song and story. Orkney and Shetland have a kind of fame as being the parts of Britain nearest to the North Pole. But there is a small number of islands neither to the north nor to the west which have played their part in Scottish history, and which are familiar to every inhabitant of the capital of Scotland, though they are seldom spoken of outside this country. These are the islands in and just at the mouth of the Firth of Forth. Some of them are now taken over by the military. Some do no more than contain a lighthouse-keeper and his family. Some have completely lost caste by becoming nothing but supports for the legs of the Forth Bridge. One, the Bass, still maintains its lonely dignity, standing off the Lothian coast like an Edinburgh Castle rock thrown into the sea.

At least one Edinburgh citizen looks upon these islands with an affectionate respect. They have formed a part of the landscape (or should it be seascape?) which he has enjoyed at home since he was a boy. He cannot think of Scotland without thinking of Edinburgh, and he cannot recall Edinburgh without remembering these grey lumps, specks and, when near at hand, precipitate rocks that are the "islands of the Forth". They, too, have their place, and an honourable place, amongst the two thousand and more Scottish islands.

VI

"SCOTLAND has a great many noble wild prospects." This statement produced the famous and characteristic, but probably good-humoured, retort from Dr. Johnson that "the noblest prospect which a Scotsman ever sees is the high road that leads him to England." Nevertheless, poor, pawky Mr. Ogilvie, who was responsible for the original remark and who received the classic buffet, was right. Scotland abounds in noble prospects. Rock, sea, mountain, moorland and plain have combined to fill this small northern country with as large a number of romantic, satisfying, exciting and indeed noble vistas and views as you could wish to find in Europe.

Man, with considerably varying success, and by means of his building, has tried to take advantage of these noble prospects. He has placed his castles on the tops of great rocks or at the end of bold promontories. He has put his Border keeps where they can survey miles of countryside. He has built his Highland fortresses at the heads of glens or of sea-lochs, or in guardian fashion at their mouths. Such few palaces as Scotland possesses are in fruitful plains or on islands in the middle of lochs. Her towns and villages, where they have not been built to command or take advantage of sea-entrances to the Kingdom, have grown up in the shadow of great things, mountains, hills and high embattled rocks.

Sometimes this form of building has been almost wholly successful. Edinburgh, for instance, is at once one of the most romantic and yet satisfying cities in the world. Her castle-crowned rock, her medieval Old Town straggling down the slope of that rock, her Augustan New Town, her guardian hills, the sea at her gates, these and many other things about her make her something more than the capital of a small country now joined to a more powerful neighbour. In appearance at least Edinburgh is amongst the first cities in Europe.

Sometimes the romantic scenery in Scotland, and the very nobility of the prospects, have tempted man to excesses unworthy of the surroundings. As soon as the Romantic Movement began to make itself felt in Scotland, architects tended to try to rival or at least decorate the fashionably romantic scenery of the country. It is for this reason that you will find in Scotland some of the very worst pseudo-romantic buildings of the nineteenth century. "Scottish Baronial" might once have been a dignified and adequate description for a native and partly French form of Scottish architecture—the buildings of the country nobility of the sixteenth and seventeenth centuries. It has now, because of the countless *pastiches* put up all over Scotland in imitation of the style in Victorian times, become an architectural term of abuse, or at best a joke, like "mock Gothic" in England. In Scotland, however, the word mock is omitted, and the whole style of building is condemned in the phrase because of the architectural abuses which have been committed in its name.

Mock Gothic was first taken up in England in the last century, and with enthusiasm, by the architects of churches and later by the builders of suburbs. So in Scotland Scottish Baronial in Victorian times began, in imitation of Balmoral, in elevated country circles, places where landowners felt the necessity of living up to the romantic traditions of the Scottish landscape. From these beginnings it also spread to the suburbs; and there can be no Scottish town that does not have in its outskirts at least a few of those turreted and crenellated monstrosities which are worse than anything that the Romantic Movement produced in the South.

The Victorian mock-Scottish-Baronial castles are now, for the most part, abandoned. Modern taste has rebelled against them; but, even if it had not, modern pockets could not afford to support them. Some of them have been pulled down, some are falling gauntly and hideously into decay, and some struggle to keep alive as hotels. The same fate is overtaking the Scottish Baronial suburbs of the towns in Scotland.

The passing away of this fashion, the deliberate removal of this junk left over from an age that became suddenly wealthy and suddenly romantic at the same time, has turned men's eyes backwards to see what we had in the way of building in Scotland before the Victorian rot set in. At no time has there been a keener interest in the genuine, the true past buildings of Scotland, the architecture which our forefathers built not only for the decoration of the face of Scotland but for their own use.

It must be admitted that before the eighteenth century there was in Scotland very little domestic architecture worthy of the name. The traveller coming north into the country for the first time misses in the smaller Scottish towns and villages that pleasant sense he has in England that these places have grown up naturally with the passing of the centuries. The average Border town or village may seem to him a grim place, not only on account of the all-pervading greyness of the stone, but because of the regulated streets, the regimented houses, the appearance of everything having been built as recently as in the last century, or at the earliest at the end of the eighteenth.

Later on, if he stays long enough to look around him, he will discover in the hidden vennels, the wynds and closes, visible signs of an earlier, a medieval, a strangely foreign-looking past in the quieter Scottish country towns. But he will have to look for that past, it will not come out and envelop him in a Washington Irving-like or Dickensian manner as in England. The reason is that the domestic architecture of these towns was originally small, insignificant, poor, and was, for the most part, overlaid or swept away when Scotland's smaller merchants, farmers and professional men grew richer after two hundred years ago and were able to build proper houses.

It is fortunate that some of this building did take place in an era of good taste—the latter half of the eighteenth century. The New Town of Edinburgh is, in Scotland, the supreme example, but there are other signs of this piece of good luck in timing for Scottish architecture in nearly every small town. Indeed it would be safe to say that in all Scottish townships that have any roots in the past of the country, and that have not been crushed out of shape by the industrial revolution, you will find at least one graceful Georgian or Regency square, crescent, street or arrangement of buildings that owes its origins to Scotland's increased prosperity in the age of taste.

Sometimes you will find considerably more than a mere relic of this. There are little towns in the north-east which have not had much occasion to grow since 1830 or thereabouts, and where the magnificently durable local stone has lasted to so good an effect that you feel that hardly anything has altered since the last wave of the Augustan age washed up this pleasant little example of town planning in the far north about a hundred and fifty years ago.

The style of this Georgian and Regency domestic and small town building in Scotland is, of course, derived from a common European stock (though it should not be forgotten that Scottish architects, the brothers Adam, contributed to that stock outside Scotland), but there is a distinctly Scottish flavour about even the most classically formal little Scottish town hall or dwelling-place. It may be, as I have already mentioned, something in the solid durability of the stone, or it may be that the architects of Scotland's brief, formal age in building designed their houses in a solid matter-of-fact way, but there is a downright, built-to-last quality in these small town houses, squares and streets which proclaims their Scottishness. Wherever you go all over Scotland you will seem to find traces of the obviously Scottish "New Town" of her capital, Edinburgh.

Before this short, prosperous and classical period that as it were, cleaned up Scotland's smaller and domestic architecture, and set it on a new footing, nearly all the native building that truly decorated the face of Scotland came from grander sources. It is true that there are some charming sixteenth- and seventeenth-century small buildings in Fife, Aberdeenshire and in the Lothians that are designed under the Dutch style, and that owe their origin to the trade that passed between Scotland and the Low Countries before the Union of Parliaments in 1707. It is true that in Galloway and in the Borders there are a certain number of churches, small municipal buildings and houses that are native to Scotland in their style (or occasionally derived from France), and were put up well before the Scottish classical revival of the eighteenth century. This smaller and earlier Scottish architecture, however, is

27   The ruined west front of Elgin Cathedral

28 The south front of Dunblane Cathedral, Perthshire

rare. And the mere fact that relics of it are now often carefully guarded as if they were museum pieces underlines this fact.

The grander sources from which the vast majority of Scottish architecture came before the eighteenth century were either ecclesiastical or noble. For only the Church or the nobility, and sometimes the landed gentry, were able to afford in Scotland buildings that were designed for long-standing purposes, and which, it was hoped, would outlast their age. Only the churchmen or the nobility were able, or indeed wished, to build for posterity.

Earlier Scottish ecclesiastical architecture has, of course, suffered from the rage and zeal of the Reformers. But with the exception of St. Andrews, there never were in Scotland great cathedrals that in style, size or magnificence could rival those in England and on the continent of Europe. Nevertheless, Arbroath, Dunkeld, Elgin, St. Giles's in Edinburgh, Glasgow Cathedral, as well as the Border abbeys and other historic churches must have seemed to Scotsmen, at the time in which they were built, impressive outward and visible signs of the Church's power and international greatness.

Today we can have but a small impression of the effect those more important church buildings produced on the face of Scotland in their day. After the massive and beautiful cathedrals of England—beginning so soon after the Border at Durham—what remains of the pre-Reformation architecture in Scotland sometimes seems small and squat. There are, of course, lovely relics which can give one some distant idea of the meticulous care the carvers and builders took in putting up these "prayers in stone" on the soil of Scotland, but, even with a full stretch of the imagination, one feels the lack of soaring ambition which animates so strongly the architecture of the Middle Ages in southern and richer lands.

The destructive energies of the Reformers, combined with the decay into which the buildings were allowed to fall in the latter half of the seventeenth and throughout the whole of the eighteenth centuries, have made it even more difficult for us to see the earlier Scottish church building as it was. The reformers were not content, as in England, to eject the statues and images of Saints and to expel the smaller signs of "Popery", they did their best to pull down whole buildings. Glasgow Cathedral, it is true, they left almost whole, but St. Andrews they, and the subsequent years of neglect, all but destroyed completely.

And so it happens that one must admit the sad fact that a large part of pre-Reformation church architecture in Scotland has also joined the "museum piece" class. The cathedrals have, for the most part, been so badly destroyed that what remains of them has been fenced round or else they have been so much added to and rebuilt that they have lost nearly all their original style. The ecclesiastical architecture that used to decorate the face of Scotland offers us many examples of half-destroyed beauty and can provoke an atmosphere of melancholy reflection, but it

97

cannot be said to play any part in decorating the appearance of the country or of showing how the life of Scotland flowed continuously down the centuries. What does remain of it only serves to show how violent was the break that occurred in the religious life of the country four hundred years ago.

On the other hand, the Baronial or architecture of the nobles of past centuries has been much better preserved. The Scottish nobles may have been a warlike lot, and they were certainly not averse to burning down, pillaging and destroying each other's castles and dwelling-places, but there has never been a social revolution in Scotland to compare with the religious revolution of the Reformation. It never was to the interest of a whole class in power to uproot and destroy the entire upper fabric of society and to wipe out the memory of it by pulling down the buildings that had housed that society and by which it was remembered.

The result is that Scotland is still fortunately rich, far richer than most people realize, in seventeenth-, sixteenth-, fifteenth-century, and even earlier, architecture of the once ruling classes. Some of this Baronial architecture still exists in the Highlands and in the West. The best examples of it, however, are to be found in Aberdeenshire and on the eastern ridge generally.

The purpose of this "upper class" architecture in the past in Scotland was, until as recently as the beginning of the eighteenth century, as much defensive as it was for the housing of its inhabitants. Hence it comes that many a nobleman's house built or reconstructed even after the Union of the Crowns in 1603 shows signs of being a fortress as well as a dwelling-place.

Nevertheless, the builders of these castles, these lesser noble country houses, were not solely concerned with practical matters. They kept an eye, as far as they could, and as far as they were allowed to, on matters of style, appearance and of beauty. For this they looked, not to their immediate neighbours, in England, but across the seas to France. No one who has toured the châteaux districts of the Loire and who has subsequently turned his attention to the vigorous remnants of the strange tall white buildings of the Scottish Renaissance—centuries can fail to notice the French influence in the more important of the old Scottish buildings.

These Scottish Renaissance castles may have seemed weighty, impressive and large to those who built them and to those who originally lived in them. By modern standards, however, they are small, and often even compact. As compared with the false Scottish-Baronial-style buildings of the last century they are, if not highly economical in the modern sense, at least manageable. This has fortunately encouraged their survival into our present age, not as museum pieces but as real living examples of architecture that can be used to the present day. Old families are still often able to keep the true inheritances of their more distant past going, when their neighbours have been obliged to sell or pull down the grandiose buildings put up by their grandfathers only a hundred years ago.

29   Evening sunlight at Gairloch, Ross and Cromarty

30 The slopes of Hart Fell from near the Devil's Beef Tub, Moffat, Dumfriesshire

No chapter on the buildings of Scotland would be complete without a reference to the small white houses of the remoter countryside, both in the Highlands and those in the moorlands of the Lowlands. These farmhouses, crofts, manses or small rural churches and meeting-places have been built in lonely places and utterly without pretensions. Their sole purpose has been to accommodate humble people working on the land, or to provide shelter where men, women and children in scattered districts could come together to worship, to discuss their affairs or to seek hospitality. Nevertheless, these white-harled or white-painted houses dotted over the Scottish landscape have for centuries become so much a part of that landscape that no Scot away from home could recall in imagination the sight of the Scottish countryside without thinking of them. They have a quiet beauty all their own. Their lines are simple, and their colour is always and miraculously purely white.

One does not know what it was that led these simple and often poor people out of the Scottish past, and living in the remoter parts of the Scottish countryside, to choose, almost without exception, to paint or harl the outside of their houses in white. In many instances it must surely have seemed easier to have left the grey stones or grey and darker-coloured building materials uncovered. White, however, was the colouring and the covering which they chose for their domestic and more rural building from the extreme north of Sutherland and Caithness down to the lonelier parts of the Border country. Maybe the small farmer or crofter found it useful to have his little dwelling-place made visible from a long distance on the wide moor by being covered in white on the outside. Or there may have been other reasons of economy or usefulness of which we know nothing.

Maybe, and this is just possible, there was a touch of aesthetic satisfaction in seeing the cleanliness and neatness of home proclaimed from the outside walls of that home. For those of us, however, who come long after the original builders of these humble houses and meeting-places, there can be no doubt. The white that they chose is not only satisfying but perfect. It is the only invariably correct shade and colouring for all circumstances within the huge framework of our Scottish hills and moorland. White is the only safe and satisfactory colour you can place against a background which on one day may be entirely grey, and which on the next may present a blaze of multi-colour that can, for sheer splendour, rival anything that the islands and the coasts and the mountains of the Mediterranean can display.

VII

ALL over the British Isles the one certain thing about the weather is that it is, and always will be, uncertain, unreliable and capricious. It is for this reason, of course, that all over the British Isles the weather remains an unfailing topic of conversation, and, for much of the year, a regular target of abuse. Nowhere in Britain, however, is it more constantly discussed or more consistently and ruefully abused than in Scotland. The result has been that the Scottish weather, like the Aberdonians' alleged meanness, has become something of an international joke. Unlike the Aberdeen joke, however, it is not a home-made article of humour primarily intended for foreign consumption; for there is a basis of truth in it, and, as we in Scotland are bound to admit, our weather can be extremely disagreeable and uncomfortable—more spectacularly disagreeable and more painfully uncomfortable than anything in the way that England can provide, with the possible exception of a London fog.

Scotland's bad-weather reputation does not, I think, spring entirely from these disagreeable and painful spells. It is also accounted for by the fact that the weather is even more unreliable for much, though not for all, of the year than it is in England, and that its unreliability is often particularly manifest during those times which in the south are usually looked upon as safe holiday periods, late July to mid-September.

But there is one other factor which, in fairness, ought to be credited to the favour of Scotland's climate, but which, in the paradoxical nature of things, often tells against it. This is simply that the weather in Scotland *can* provide glorious spells during which the beauty of Scotland is shown to such spectacular advantage that when the inevitable bad weather does come it is such a disappointment that it seems even worse than it is. This disappointment is heightened by the unreliability of it all. Scotland is admittedly a country of scenic extremes. It contains some of the loveliest countryside in Europe and some of the ugliest; but the visitor to Scotland can in this matter at least make his own choice. He can go to the beautiful parts of Scotland and avoid the ugly ones. He cannot do this with the weather. And if he has had experience of a beautiful part of Scotland in beautiful weather, or has heard of other people's experiences, and strikes later on a really bad patch of the Scottish climate at its worst, he forgets the good and remembers only the bad.

The truth is that the weather in Scotland presents a rich diversity which suits the diversity of the country as a whole, and it must be taken, suffered and enjoyed as a rich diversity. This is easy enough counsel to give, but it is not so easy to follow. Even the most hardened inhabitants of Scotland never quite get over the surprises that their country's climate annually has in store for them. And if this be true of the natives themselves (as their regular conversation proves) one can hardly blame the occasional incomer from the south for being puzzled by, and a little apprehensive of, it.

The chief complaint against the Scottish climate is based not on its severity but on its wetness and windiness. And it would be difficult for even the most fervid patriot to put up much of a defence against such charges after, let us say, a long spell of Glasgow mists and rain, or of that most painful of all climatic experiences in Scotland, an early spring in Edinburgh blasted by the east winds. Let us admit, therefore, that there is no question but that the West of Scotland from Cape Wrath down to the Mull of Galloway can for long periods be very wet and rainy, and that the East of Scotland for its whole length can be equally at the mercy of the winds from the North Sea. Having made this admission, and before we come to consider the better, the truly good and equally truly Scottish weather that both East and West *can* provide, let it also be pointed out that, at the worst, Edinburgh and the East has not a damp climate, and Glasgow and the West has not a cold one.

To the discomfort of western wetness and eastern windiness, there must, at least for the stranger to Scotland, be added the fact that both wet and wind can and frequently do occur at unseasonable times of the year. Glasgow and the West, after a long and temptingly beneficent spring, can provide a late June, July and August of depressing dampness. Those of us who live in Edinburgh and the East may have just reached that stage of the year when we feel that we can safely congratulate ourselves on having passed through a really mild winter, when the winds not only of March but of April and even of May can come to blast our hopes; and we somehow manage to stumble through to the comparative security of an East of Scotland summer embittered by the knowledge that we have been cheated of spring.

Ah! but all the irritations, frustrations and disappointments that the Scottish weather is so often responsible for can be obliterated and forgotten by the enjoyment of one of those long spells when our climate suddenly decides to be as generous as heretofore it has been capricious. Spring in the West Highlands is about as reliable a season in that part of Scotland as exists. And anyone who has felt and seen the approach of the longer, warmer summer days during a whole month coming in from the Atlantic and enlivening and enriching the whole lovely scene will feel that he can forgive Scotland for anything she may do for the rest of the year for the sake of that one month. I have said coming in from the Atlantic, for that is exactly what the spring seems to do in the West Highlands. And it is all the more enchanting in that it is from that same quarter and from over those same waters that the cruellest and most depressing of the winter storms were wont to come.

Anyone, too, who has been fortunate enough to be in the far North during a long spell of midsummer fine weather will soon put out of mind or forgive the ardour and discomforts of the early year in the South. Late June and early July in Caithness, the North-West Highlands, or, perhaps best of all, in Shetland, can be an experience that no one who passes his ordinary existence elsewhere in the British Isles is likely ever to forget. Time, to use a hackneyed but in this instance inevitable phrase, seems to stand still. Days melt into each other with the interval of no more than twilight to divide them. The whole atmosphere of morning, high noon, evening and the last hour of day is filled with that long slanting light which can only be found in the North and which is the subtlest influence upon colour in the world. Add to this length of days spent in the lengthening light, the effect of the wide, the apparently limitless, horizons of the North Atlantic, and you have the feeling that you are suspended in a soft illumination that will never come to an end.

Exquisite though these seasons, spring in the West Highlands and high summer in the far North may be, they give place, for me at least, to a fine autumn anywhere in Scotland, yes, literally anywhere in the true countryside. For autumn is our true, our best Scottish time of the year, and is, all over the country, more dependable than any other season.

Autumn is the time when Scotland as a whole repents of the fact, though she may have given us a lovely spring in the west, she has cheated us of it in the East and North, that though she may have been prodigal of her long days of light in the far North at midsummer, she has drenched the Clyde and the nearer West Highlands throughout June and July. In October, and even deep into November, she is able to pull herself together all over the country and to make amends. She can indeed make these autumnal amends to such purpose that sometimes half of the winter season has been invaded and conquered by the dying year's late beneficence; and we come to the very edge of Christmas and the New Year with the comfortable reflection that we are actually into the time of the lengthening days without having tasted anything of the severity of winter.

A large part of the beauty of a truly fine Scottish autumn lies in its stillness. After the equinoctial gales have howled, roared, broken and shouted their say in late September, there often ensues a period of dead calm which will last for weeks. This calm is accompanied by pale-gold sunshine, and the very softest of mists which does not obscure the view to any distance, but merely gives a general delicacy to the colouring.

And what colouring there is in the Scottish autumn! As elsewhere, in the south of Britain, the gold of the changing trees is magnificent; but in Scotland the green leaves last longer, with the gold reminding us that the year is far from dead yet. I have seen the blood-red of fuchsia in Skye as late as November; and even in the

31   The lighthouse and harbour at Macduff, Banffshire

32   The harbour at Stonehaven, Aberdeenshire

harsher East the colours of the wild flowers last late in sheltered places once the great storms are over. The celebrated purple of the heather is, of course, an early autumnal colour; but it is not one of my favourite adornments of the Scottish scene, though it has its admirers. Bracken may be a pernicious plant, but I prefer the colour of bracken to that of heather. The gold of a bracken-covered hill in autumn lying under a blue sky is a sight not easily forgotten. Recently I spent most of October and November riding a hill pony from the East Lowlands to the North-West Highlands. It was the ideal way of travelling in such a season, and through such country. I can honestly say that in all my experience of the colours of nature, I have never had so prolonged, so rich or so varied a feast.

I have mentioned earlier the wonderful effect of the long slanting light at mid-summer in the far North. But the beauty of the northern light is not confined in Scotland to the end of June nor to the northern islands. It can display itself in springtime, in late summer, even in winter, and particularly in autumn. And it is to be seen in Edinburgh, on the Clyde and in the Borders, as well as in the islands of Shetland. The main quality of its outstanding beauty when it is at its best is the luminosity which it seems to give to the objects which it touches. This luminosity arises from the fact that the light comes over the horizon at an oblique angle and does not fall directly upon the scene. It therefore draws the colours gently out of everything which it gently illuminates, so that everything that you can see seems to have light in itself which it gives out of itself.

I have written of the northern light, which is the greatest benison of the Scottish climate, before. I wrote about it when my theme was the capital of Scotland. I do not think I can improve on what I had to say there. What I said then is true now and it can be true of the Scottish scene from Berwick or Dumfries to Lerwick in the ultimate isles. This is what I wrote:

"This then is her" [Edinburgh's] "supreme gift to the painter, the architect, the artist, indeed to all men of sensibility who take pleasure in contemplating her. It is truly Edinburgh's gift to her admirers, for it is generously as well as gently bestowed. In Italy and in Provencal France they can show you sunflowers and fruits and white walls and painted walls that gloriously throw back the light that is so gloriously thrown upon them. But in our Northern climate we do not throw back the light at you; for we could not. We have not that kind of luminary strength. Instead we give it to you, give it out of our own earth, stone, sky, sea and air."